the JUICE SOLUTION

ERIN QUON ✚
BRIANA STOCKTON

PHOTOGRAPHS BY
SARA REMINGTON

weldonowen

ENERGIZE

Chapter One

Light, refreshing juices, packed
with fruits and herbs that energize
and kick-start your metabolism

PAGE 22

FUEL

Chapter Two

Dense, filling, meal-like
juices loaded with vitamins,
fiber, and healthy fats

PAGE 44

DETOX

Chapter Three

Detoxifying juices full of
naturally cleansing vegetables,
fruits, and whole raw spices

PAGE 64

PROTECT

Chapter Four

Vitamin- and mineral-rich
juices that help strengthen your
immune system naturally

PAGE 86

All About
JUICING

Drinking fresh fruit and vegetable juices is a simple, healthy way to ensure you're getting the vitamins and minerals you need for a balanced diet. Liquefying fruits and vegetables in a masticating or centrifugal home juicer makes consuming large amounts of produce easy, delicious, and gentle on the digestive system.

The benefits of juicing are endless: energizing naturally; replacing meals with wholesome, easy-to-digest ingredients; detoxifying your system; and enhancing your immunity, among many others. In addition, drinking healthy juices can help you form easy, healthy eating habits and may help combat health problems. Some regular juicers claim that juicing even helps with weight loss.

We've organized this book into four main chapters for different needs throughout the day: light, energizing juices to start your morning and rev up your metabolism; denser, fibrous juices to fuel you or stand in as a light meal; cleansing juices with diuretic properties to detoxify your body; and antioxidant-, antibacterial-, and anti-inflammatory-rich drinks to protect your body from illness and combat dehydration.

Whether you've never juiced before or like to do juice cleanses regularly, turn the page to discover all the tips, tricks, and knowledge you need.

There's so much to love about juicing—it's healthful, hydrating, energizing, and the flavor combinations are endless. It's the proverbial golden ticket to fueling your body with mouth-watering, tasty, healthy nutrients. Juicing came into our lives in different ways (Erin was inspired by friends who juiced and Briana, a juicer for over 6 years, found that juicing complemented her raw lifestyle). Once we experienced the benefits in these vitamin-loaded juices, we were hooked! When we realized how much we were spending on bottled juices, which can sometimes contain fillers, like high-moisture lettuce or excess water, we knew it was time to start making juices at home. Electric juicers seemed pricey at first, until we realized we were not just investing in the machine, but also a healthy lifestyle.

People ask us why we juice, and the simplest answer is that it's just part of our lifestyle. (For Erin, her mornings begin with juicing for her family: anything from simple, fresh orange juice to kale and beet concoctions. For Briana, juicing is part of her daily schedule: enjoyed in the morning, after a work out, or before a client meeting.) Both of our jobs require a lot of time on our feet, and juicing helps keep us hydrated and energized for long, taxing workdays. It also helps us stay energized throughout the day, so that we can give 100 percent to all our clients. But juicing isn't just a solution for energy—it's a simple way to reboot our bodies and build our immune systems while on the run.

We're so excited to share the recipes in this book, because they replenish your body with vitamins and minerals, rehydrate you, and taste delicious. We've learned that a few bucks at the farmers' market goes a long way in providing a week's worth of juices. In fact, juicing at home, as opposed to buying the bottled stuff, gets you double for your money: You not only get a delicious juice, but you also get the dehydrated fiber, or pulp, that's left behind. We've discovered so many great uses for it: We use vegetable fiber for the base of stocks or in muffins; we sprinkle nut fiber over salads or use it in cookies; we add fruit and vegetable fiber to dog food; and many other ideas.

We hope you'll feel inspired by the enticing juices within this book. We hand-selected our favorite juice recipes—the same ones we drink everyday to keep us healthy, energized, and hydrated through long days of personal training and cooking—for you to enjoy at home. Even though we've included over 90 recipes, we encourage you to keep experimenting—you'll be surprised at how good even the wildest of combinations can taste. The beauty of the juicing lifestyle is that you can't go wrong: at the end of the day, you've hydrated your body with essential nutrients, and that's what's important.

Why, When & How to Juice

Why There are endless reasons to juice: to improve health, increase energy, lose weight, prevent diseases, and more. While we can't guarantee any of these results, we can say that incorporating juices into your everyday life is a positive step for your wellbeing. Adding just one juice in the morning supplies more nutrients than some people consume in a whole a day. In addition, juicing provides a simplified way of preparing and consuming all your favorite produce. It's a healthy, refreshing, and fast way to fulfill your body's dietary needs.

When Deciding when to juice is up to you. Since juicing is a great way to deliver a nutrient boost, incorporating a juice into your breakfast plan is a smart start and can boost your energy without the aid of caffeine. If you want a quick, easy, and healthy meal-on-the go, there are lots of juices that are bolstered with healthy fats and fiber to keep you satisfied. If you're preparing for a mentally or physically challenging activity, like travel, an important exam, or a sports competition, there are juices to help build your immune system. If you've overindulged in food or alcohol, there are juices to help flush toxins out of your system. Over time, you'll grow to enjoy these juices so much, you'll drink them just because you feel like it!

How Juicing requires a certain level of commitment, but the long-term payoff for your health is well worth it. First, you'll need to invest in a juicer. We've created a chart on pages 12–13 to help you pick a home juicer that's right for you. Next, in order to get the most out of your juicer, it's helpful to maintain a fresh supply of fruits and vegetables. Having an abundance and variety of produce on hand means fulfilling any craving or health need in seconds. If you have a busy schedule, you may find juicing easier and even more enjoyable when you have an abundance of juices within arm's reach. Most juices will stay fresh for up to 3 days in the refrigerator, or for longer in the freezer, so you can plan ahead if you have a busy schedule. (Frozen juices need a few hours in the refrigerator to thaw.) Finally, start experimenting! By mixing and matching ingredients, you'll soon learn what tastes and feels good to you.

About CLEANSING

A juice cleanse generally refers to a meal plan where whole foods are replaced by nutrient-dense juices up to 5 times a day. Such cleanses are touted as ways to give the digestive system a break, recharge your body with an influx of vitamins and minerals, and, sometimes, to lose weight. If you're thinking about cleansing, it's important to first consult your doctor or a nutritionist and map out a plan that's best suited to your health needs and personal goals. Juice cleansing isn't for everyone, especially young children and pregnant women, and there's no guarantee of health gain or weight loss results. If you're looking to begin a low-risk cleanse, start by replacing one meal or snack a day with a juice. Make sure to include a variety of soft and hard vegetables and fruit to ensure you're getting a balanced meal in place of your solid one.

Choosing a Juicer

Buying a juicer can be confusing—there are many different models on the market, each touting different features and benefits. This guide differentiates between the two most popular juicer models: a slow-masticating juicer and a centrifugal juicer. Below we explain the difference between these types of juicers and the pros and cons of each, to help you decide which model is best suited to your juicing needs.

Slow-Masticating Juicer

A two-stage, low-speed system first crushes the food, and then presses it to ensure a high juice yield without aerating the juice.

FEATURES AND BENEFITS:

The juicing process takes a few seconds longer than with a centrifugal juicer

Produces less heat than a centrifugal juicer, therefore preserving more natural enzymes

For the highest juice yield, cut ingredients into 2-inch (5-cm) pieces

Many models let you customize the amount of pulp and fiber in your juice

Slow operating speed reduces chance of oxidation (when juice loses some of its natural color) and separation (froth on top and layering of juice ingredients)

Delivers 35% more juice and maintains up to 60% more vitamins from certain types of fresh produce, such as herbs and leafy greens, than traditional centrifugal models

Some models make smoothies as well as juice

Centrifugal Juicer

A fast spinning motion shreds ingredients into a pulp, and then extracts the juice from the pulp with centrifugal force.

FEATURES AND BENEFITS:

Juice is extracted almost instantly, which is helpful for a busy schedule

Models with a wide feeding tube mean many ingredients don't need to be pre-cut

Some models boast two speeds: low for softer ingredients, high for firmer ingredients

High operating speed means some oxidation (when juice loses some of its natural color) and separation (froth on top and layering of juice ingredients) can occur

Extracts the most juice from soft, high-moisture ingredients and extracts less juice from fibrous and leafy ingredients

Centrifugal models are generally more affordable than slow-masticating models

Caring for YOUR JUICER

Make the most of your equipment and fresh fruits and vegetables by keeping your juicer in top shape. An improperly functioning juicer may waste raw ingredients and won't produce the maximum amount of juice possible. If you're making multiple servings of juice, run a cup or two of water through the machine after each batch. Be careful not to overload your juicer. For best results, consult the owner's manual for your juicer to discover the right way to work with ingredients in your machine.

Getting to Know the Machine

Once you've decided which juicer works best for you, spend some time learning about its use and features. A great way to do that is to take it apart. Understanding your juicer's design also helps prevent future problems. Juicers are comprised of multiple pieces that work in a system to extract liquid from produce and separate the pulp. Since each juicer is comprised of different pieces, consult your user's manual for the correct way to work with it.

The three universal components of any juicer are the food chute, the juice spout, and the pulp spout. Before you start, prep your ingredients (trim, wash, and cut, if necessary) and set them on the counter near the juicer. Have ready the vessels for collecting the juice and pulp as directed for your juicer. If you have a model with an open-and-close mechanism on the juice spout, make sure it's open before operating the machine for juice. To begin the juicing cycle, drop the prepped produce down the food chute, alternating fibrous and juicy ingredients. Some models are equipped with a pusher to help ease the fruit and vegetables into the machine. Next, wait for the extracted juice to emerge from the juice spout and, for juicer models with an external pulp collector, the extracted pulp to be pushed out of the opposite end. Finally, clean the machine according to the manufacturer's instructions as soon as possible after use.

The best way to get to know your juicer, and get the most out of your investment, is to use it a lot. Use the recipes in these pages as inspiration, then experiment with different flavors, colors, and textures. Test the settings (such as fine or coarse strainers for slow-masticating juicers or machine speeds for centrifugal juicers) to determine if you prefer your juices on the finer or the pulpier side. Experiment (within reason) by using different parts of the fruit or vegetable, as long as they are considered edible. For more on working with ingredients, turn to page 17.

A good way to discover juice combinations you really enjoy is to make a few different glasses of single ingredient juices, and then experiment by combining the juices in small portions. This allows you to discover new favorite flavors without wasting too much.

How to Prep Ingredients for Juicing

Prepping juice ingredients usually involves simply washing the produce and cutting it to fit the food chute of your machine. Here are some additional tips for popular fruits and vegetables.

Wash whole ingredients to rid them of dirt or grit. Use a produce brush to remove stubborn, caked-on dirt.

Pare away tough skins: Anything with an inedible or bitter peel, such as those on avocados and citrus, should be removed. Any peel you choose to keep intact should be thoroughly scrubbed and washed.

Remove any inedible pits. This is especially important for stone fruits, such as cherries and peaches. Small, soft seeds, like those in apples, pears, and citrus can be juiced. Papaya seeds can be juiced for extra nutrients.

Place leafy greens and herbs in a colander and plunge them into a cold-water bath. Swirl them around to remove dirt. Drain, and repeat if necessary for extra-dirty greens.

For added nutrients, keep the leafy tops of vegetables and fruits intact. This includes strawberry stems, beet greens, carrot tops, fennel fronds, and celery leaves.

Nuts should be soaked in water for a minimum of 5 hours, but preferably 8 hours, before being juiced into milk.

The way you prep ingredients for juicing can affect the taste of the finished juice. For example, juicing citrus with and without its peel has a very different result.

Some recipes call for a "knob of ginger," which refers to a 1-inch (2.5-cm) piece of fresh ginger. Peeling is optional.

Some recipes call for fresh turmeric, which resembles a small piece of ginger. It can be found at many farmer's markets and health food stores. Peeling is optional.

Some ingredients, such as coconut water, coconut oil, chia seeds, and others are simply stirred into the finished juice to add volume or nutrients to the juice.

About RAW HONEY

Because raw honey is unpasteurized, it's loaded in live enzymes and antimicrobial compounds known to have antibacterial properties. You can find raw honey in many grocery stores in the baking or health food aisles. Pregnant women, young children, and some people with food allergies or immune disorders should not consume raw honey. Pasteurized honey can easily replace raw honey in all these recipes.

Storing FRESH JUICE

For the freshest juice, and highest level of nutrients, aim to drink juices within 24 hours. They can be refrigerated in airtight containers or bottles for up to 72 hours. If you are using the dehydrated fiber, or pulp (see page 8 for ideas) it should also be used within 24 hours for best texture and flavor. Otherwise pulp can be frozen and reserved for future use.

Tips and Tricks for Juicing

One of the joys of juicing is the flavor options are endless. No matter the combination, if juice is made from fresh fruit or vegetables, you're doing your body a big, nutritious favor. Here are some good tips to keep in mind while experimenting.

Combine Hues

The more diverse the colors that go into the juice, the more nutritious, and hopefully delicious, it will be—even if the end result is a little brownish in color.

Color Matters

Studies show that humans are more satisfied by visually appealing food. If your juice is an off-color, consider adding an ingredient with a strong hue, such as red beets, orange carrots, or leafy greens. The addition of lemon juice helps retain bright juice colors.

Think of it as a Meal

Not sure what to combine to get a taste you like? Juice items that you would want to eat together in their whole form. Think of your favorite items to put in a salad or eat as a snack, and let that be the inspiration for your juice.

Mix Textures

Combining soft, juicy produce (such as pears, cucumbers, and citrus) with fibrous, firm produce (such as kale, root vegetables, and nuts) makes a well-balanced juice. Because fibrous ingredients produce less liquid, it's important to combine them with moisture-rich ingredients. Otherwise, you'll end up using pounds of fibrous ingredients to fill up one glass.

Taste as You Go

You can make your mixed juices by alternating ingredients in the machine, or you can collect each juiced item individually and combine the juices afterward. If you're using the former technique, try your juice after each addition, to see if it needs more of a certain ingredient or something new.

Clean Out the Fridge

Use juicing as an opportunity to not only clean out the vegetable bin and fruit bowl, but also to encourage you to keep them regularly stocked.

Freezing Juice

Most juices will last for a few days in the freezer. When you're ready to consume a frozen juice, thaw it for several hours in the refrigerator until it returns to a liquid state.

ENERGIZE

In This Chapter

juices that
ENERGIZE

❧

Energizing juices, packed with vibrant fruits and light vegetables, are a great way to start your day or supply a midday pick-me-up. Instead of reaching for the usual morning coffee, wake up your taste buds with a metabolism-boosting, energizing juice. These juices are as clean, pure, and simple as they get. Because they're extracted from ingredients with a high water density and low fiber content, they're easy for your digestive system to handle in the morning (your body is known to be in elimination cycle from the early morning until noon, and these types of juices will enhance the body's natural processes). These are the lightest juices featured in this book, so they're best enjoyed followed by a breakfast shake, healthful solid foods, or a denser mid-afternoon juice.

Among the standout ingredients of the juices in this chapter, tropical fruits and citrus lend a whopping amount of energy-boosting vitamin C. It's no surprise that consuming vitamin C is a great way to start your day, but these juices go beyond the famed orange juice breakfast. Apples are added to help regulate blood sugar and boost a healthy gut. Grapes bring numerous health benefits, including substances to help combat fatigue and deliver powerful antioxidants. Fresh mint is a natural stimulant, which activates the salivary glands and promotes digestion. These are just a few of the ingredients that help give a good start to your day.

For more on ingredients that energize, turn to page 26.

energizing INGREDIENTS

mangoes

High levels of potassium can help control blood pressure and keep you feeling full for a long time. Mangoes are full of enzymes that break down protein, which helps improve digestion.

grapes

Red and black grapes are an excellent source of the antioxidant manganese, which can help regulate blood sugar. Naturally sweet in taste, grapes are surprisingly low on the glycemic index.

kiwis

Kiwis are an exceptional source of vitamin C, which is a natural energy provider. With a low glycemic index, kiwis will steady your blood sugar, helping you to feel full and satisfied over time.

pineapples

Pineapples are an excellent source of vitamin C, which is a natural energy provider. The high levels of vitamin B may help with digestion. They also contain compounds that help increase circulation.

fresh mint

The strong aroma of mint activates the salivary glands, which secrete digestive enzymes, promoting healthy digestive functions.

apples

Apples are high in quercetin, a flavonoid which slows the digestive process of carbohydrates, helping to prolong energy storage and regulate blood sugar.

Cherry-Tangerine-Apple

2 cups (12 oz/375 g) pitted
fresh sweet cherries or thawed,
frozen cherries

3 tangerines

1 green apple

Stem the cherries, if necessary.
Peel the tangerines cut the apple to
fit the juicer. Place the cherries,
tangerines, and apple into the feeder
of the juice extractor, and run the
machine. Enjoy as soon as possible.

Makes about 2 cups (16 fl oz/500 ml)

Sunrise Juice

1 small lemon

1 orange

1 papaya

1 small fresh turmeric

Knob of ginger

4 carrots

Peel the lemon, orange, and papaya
and cut to fit the juicer. Place the
lemon, orange, papaya, turmeric,
ginger, and carrots into the feeder
of the juice extractor, and run the
machine. Enjoy as soon as possible.

Makes about 2 cups (16 fl oz/500 ml)

Cherry-Berry-Apple

2 cups (12 oz/375 g) pitted
fresh sweet cherries or thawed,
frozen cherries

1 green apple

1 pt (8 oz/250 g) raspberries

1 pt (8 oz/250 g) strawberries

Stem the cherries, if necessary. Cut
the apple to fit the juicer. Place
the cherries, apple, raspberries,and
strawberries into the feeder of
the juice extractor, and run the
machine. Enjoy as soon as possible.

Makes about 2 cups (16 fl oz/500 ml)

Rise + Shine

½ cantaloupe

1 pink grapefruit

1 small yellow beet

Small knob of ginger

1 pint (8 oz/250 g) raspberries

Peel and seed the cantaloupe. Peel
the grapefruit. Cut the cantaloupe,
grapefruit, and beet to fit the juicer.
Place the cantaloupe, grapefruit, beet,
ginger, and raspberries into the feeder
of the juice extractor, and run the
machine. Enjoy as soon as possible.

Makes about 2 cups (16 fl oz/500 ml)

Pineapple-Banana-Strawberry

1 banana

½ pineapple

1 pint (8 oz/250 g) strawberries

Peel the banana. Peel the pineapple and cut it to fit the juicer. Place the banana, pineapple, and strawberries into the feeder of the juice extractor, and run the machine. Enjoy as soon as possible.

Makes about 2 cups (16 fl oz/500 ml)

Morning in the Tropics

2 mangoes

1 lime

1 papaya

1 orange

8 fresh mint leaves

Peel the mangoes and remove the pits. Peel the lime, papaya, and orange and cut to fit the juicer. Place the mango, lime, papaya, orange, and mint into the feeder of the juice extractor, and run the machine. Enjoy as soon as possible.

Makes about 2 cups (16 fl oz/500 ml)

Tropical Berry Mint

¼ pineapple

1 kiwi

1 pear

1 cup (4 oz/125 g) blackberries

30 fresh mint leaves

2 cups (8 oz/250 g) blueberries

Peel the pineapple and kiwi. Cut the pineapple and pear to fit the juicer. Place the pineapple, kiwi, pear, blackberries, mint, and blueberries into the feeder of the juice extractor, and run the machine. Enjoy as soon as possible.

Makes about 2 cups (16 fl oz/500 ml)

Minty Pick-Me-Up

1 large pineapple

1 pear

30 fresh mint leaves

1 cup (4 oz/125 g) strawberries

Peel the pineapple. Cut the pineapple and pear to fit the juicer. Place the pineapple, pear, mint, and strawberries into the feeder of the juice extractor, and run the machine. Enjoy as soon as possible.

Makes about 2½ cups (20 fl oz/625 ml)

GINGERY BEET-APPLE

3 yellow beets
1 green apple
knob of ginger

Cut the beets
and apple to fit the
juicer. Place the beet,
ginger, and apple into the
feeder of a juice extractor,
and run the machine. Enjoy
as soon as possible.

~

Makes about 2 cups
(16 fl oz/500 ml)

Apple-Nectarine-Strawberry

3 green apples

1 nectarine

½ bunch fresh parsley

1 cup (4 oz/125 g)
strawberries

Cut the apples to fit the juicer.
Cut the nectarine in half and
remove the pit. Place the apples,
nectarine, parsley, and strawberries
and into the feeder of the juice
extractor, and run the machine.
Enjoy as soon as possible.

Makes about 2 cups
(16 fl oz/500 ml)

Apple-Berry Refresher

2 green apples

5 cups (20 oz/625 g)
blackberries

Cut the apples to fit the juicer.
Place the apples and blackberries
into the feeder of the juice
extractor, and run the machine.
Enjoy as soon as possible.

Makes about 2½ cups
(20 fl oz/625 ml)

Parsley-Kiwi-Citrus

- 4 kiwis
- 2 oranges
- 1 lemon
- ½ bunch parsley

Peel the kiwis, oranges and lemon, and cut to fit the juicer. Place the kiwis, oranges, parsley, and lemon into the feeder of the juice extractor, and run the machine. Enjoy as soon as possible.

Makes about 2 cups (16 fl oz/500 ml)

Orange-Carrot-Melon

- ½ cantaloupe
- 2 oranges
- 8 carrots

Peel and seed the cantaloupe. Peel the oranges and cut the cantaloupe and oranges to fit the juicer. Place the cantaloupe, oranges, and carrots into the feeder of the juice extractor, and run the machine. Enjoy as soon as possible.

Makes about 2 cups (16 fl oz/500 ml)

Tart Watermelon

- 3 cups (15 oz/470 g) watermelon pieces
- 1 lime
- 6 stalks celery

Peel the watermelon and lime and cut to fit the juicer. Place the watermelon, lime, and celery into the feeder of the juice extractor, and run the machine. Enjoy as soon as possible.

Makes about 2 cups (16 fl oz/500 ml)

Green Day

- 3 kiwis
- 3 green apples
- 1 cucumber
- 10 fresh mint leaves

Peel the kiwis. Cut the kiwis, apples, and cucumber to fit the juicer. Place the kiwis, apples, mint, and cucumber into the feeder of the juice extractor, and run the machine. Enjoy as soon as possible.

Makes about 2 cups (16 fl oz/500 ml)

Tangy Strawberry-Grape

½ lime

4 cups (24 oz/750 g) red or purple grapes

2 cups (8 oz/250 g) strawberries

Peel the lime and cut it to fit the juicer. Place the grapes, strawberries, and lime into the feeder of the juice extractor, and run the machine. Enjoy as soon as possible.

Makes about 2 cups (16 fl oz/500 ml)

Fruit Salad

1 pink grapefruit

¼ cantaloupe

2 cups (8 oz/250 g) strawberries

1 cup (6 oz/185 g) red or purple grapes

Peel the grapefruit. Peel and seed the cantaloupe. Cut the grapefruit and cantaloupe to fit the juicer. Place the grapefruit, strawberries, cantaloupe, and grapes into the feeder of the juice extractor, and run the machine. Enjoy as soon as possible.

Makes about 2 cups (16 fl oz/500 ml)

2 bunches grapes
chia seeds

GRAPE POWER JUICE

Remove the grapes from the vine. Place the grapes into the feeder of the juice extractor, and run the machine. Pour the juice into a glass, stir in chia seeds to taste (start with about 1 tablespoon), and enjoy as soon as possible.

Makes about 2 cups
(16 fl oz/500 ml)

Green Dew

1 honeydew melon

1 lime

4 stalks celery

Peel and seed the melon. Peel the lime. Cut the melon and lime to fit the juicer. Place the lime, melon, and celery into the feeder of a juice extractor, and run the machine. Enjoy as soon as possible.

Makes about 2 cups (16 fl oz/500 ml)

Minty Pineapple-Cucumber

½ pineapple

½ lime

½ Persian cucumber

10 fresh mint leaves

1 stalk celery

Peel the pineapple and lime. Cut the pineapple, lime, and cucumber to fit the juicer. Place the pineapple, lime, cucumber, mint, and celery into the feeder of a juice extractor, and run the machine. Enjoy as soon as possible.

Makes about 2 cups (16 fl oz/500 ml)

Revitalizing Elixir

3 cups (15 oz/470 g) watermelon pieces

1 lime

1 Persian cucumber

Knob of ginger

Peel the watermelon and lime. Cut the watermelon, lime, and cucumber to fit the juicer. Place the watermelon, lime, ginger, and cucumber into the feeder of the juice extractor, and run the machine. Enjoy as soon as possible.

Makes about 2 cups (16 fl oz/500 ml)

Blue Sunshine

2 oranges

1 lemon

4 cups (24 oz/750 g) red grapes

1 cup (4 oz/125 g) blueberries

Peel the oranges and lemon and cut to fit the juicer. Place the oranges, lemon, grapes, and blueberries into the feeder of the juice extractor, and run the machine. Enjoy as soon as possible.

Makes about 2 cups (16 fl oz/500 ml)

Sunshiny Day

3 oranges

¼ cantaloupe

2 green apples

10 fresh mint leaves

Peel the oranges. Peel and seed the cantaloupe. Cut the oranges, cantaloupe, and apples to fit the juicer. Place the cantaloupe, apples, oranges, and mint into the feeder of a juice extractor, and run the machine. Enjoy as soon as possible.

Makes about 2 cups (16 fl oz/500 ml)

Mango-Apple-Pineapple

1 mango

1 pineapple

1 green apple

Peel and pit the mango. Peel the pineapple. Cut the pineapple and apple to fit the juicer. Place the mango, pineapple, and apple into the feeder of a juice extractor, and run the machine. Enjoy as soon as possible.

Makes about 2 cups (16 fl oz/500 ml)

Avocado-Kiwi-Citrus Tonic

2 oranges

1 grapefruit

1 kiwi

1 avocado

3 stalks celery

Peel the oranges, grapefruit, kiwi, and avocado. Remove the pit from the avocado. Cut the oranges and grapefruit to fit the juicer. Place the oranges, grapefruit, kiwi, avocado, and celery into the feeder of the juice extractor, and run the machine. Enjoy as soon as possible.

Makes about 2 cups (16 fl oz/500 ml)

Kickstarter

2 kiwis

2 cups (8 oz/250 g) raspberries

1 small fresh turmeric

Knob of ginger

1 cup (4 oz/125 g) strawberries

Peel the kiwis. Place the kiwis, raspberries, turmeric, ginger, and strawberries into the feeder of the juice extractor, and run the machine. Enjoy as soon as possible.

Makes about 2 cups (16 fl oz/500 ml)

FUEL

In This Chapter

fueling INGREDIENTS

nuts

Nuts are full of protein and healthy monounsaturated fat. Soak them in water and run them through the juicer for a naturally creamy, dairy-free milk. Brazil nuts are one of the best varieties for making creamy milk that's rich in healthy fats. Almonds, hazelnuts and cashews also produce delicious, subtly-sweet nut milks.

kale

Kale is bursting in beta-carotene, carotenoids, vitamin A, and calcium. It's high fiber content can help keep you feel fuller longer. If your juicer has a pulp control lever, choose the "close" setting to get pulpier juices with more fiber. Some juice aficionados like to chew pulpy green juice to help process its beneficial fiber.

sweet potatoes

The darker the flesh of a sweet potato, the richer it is in phytonutrients. These root vegetables are loaded with good carbohydrates that help stabilize blood sugar.

avocados

Creamy avocados are full of
good-for-you monounsaturated
fats, which have been shown
to aid the body's absorption
of antioxidants while also
protecting the heart and joints.
Avocados' buttery consistency
lends smoothness to juices.

chard

Chard and other leafy
greens are bursting with
calcium. Their crunchy stems
are rich in fiber, which
can help control hunger.
If your juicer has a pulp
control lever, choose the
"close" setting for pulpier
juices with more fiber.

Cran-Banana

2 bananas

1 papaya

¼ pineapple

1 cup (4 oz/125 g) cranberries

Peel the bananas, papaya, and pineapple. Cut the papaya and pineapple to fit the juicer. Place the banana, papaya, pineapple, and cranberries into the feeder of a juice extractor and run the machine. Enjoy as soon as possible.

Makes about 2 cups (16 fl oz/500 ml)

Sweet + Spicy

½ pineapple

2 small apples

1 small sweet potato

Knob of ginger

½ jalapeño

Peel the pineapple. Cut the pineapple, apples, and sweet potato to fit the juicer. Place the sweet potato, pineapple, ginger, jalapeño, and apples into the feeder of a juice extractor and run the machine. Enjoy as soon as possible.

Makes about 2 cups (16 fl oz/500 ml)

Green Dream

2 kiwis

1 lemon

1 green apple

1 Persian cucumber

½ bunch kale

½ head romaine lettuce

Peel the kiwis and lemon. Cut the kiwis, lemon, apple, and cucumber to fit the juicer. Place the kiwi, kale, lemon, romaine, cucumber, and apple into the feeder of a juice extractor, and run the machine. Enjoy as soon as possible.

Makes about 2 cups (16 fl oz/500 ml)

Pear, Apple + Greens

1 pear

1 apple

1 bunch rainbow chard

1 cup (1 oz/30 g) fresh spinach

½ bunch fresh flat-leaf parsley

Cut the pear and apple to fit the juicer. Place the chard, pear, spinach, parsley, and apple, into the feeder of a juice extractor and run the machine. Enjoy as soon as possible.

Makes about 2 cups (16 fl oz/500 ml)

3 apples
2 beets
8 kale leaves
knob of ginger

SWEET GREENS

Cut the apples and beets to fit the juicer. Place the beets, kale, ginger, and apples into the feeder of a juice extractor, and run the machine. Enjoy as soon as possible.

Makes
about 2 cups
(16 fl oz/500 ml)

Creamy Kale Juice

1 cup (8 fl oz/250 ml)
cashew milk (page 61)

2 golden beets

2 bananas

1 avocado

10 kale leaves

Make the cashew milk as directed.
Cut the beets to fit the juicer.
Peel the bananas and avocado and
remove the pit from the avocado.
Place the kale, bananas, avocado,
and beets into the feeder of
a juice extractor, and run the
machine. Pour the juice into
a glass, stir in the cashew milk,
and enjoy as soon as possible.

Makes about 2 cups
(16 fl oz/500 ml)

Carrot-Ginger + Greens

1 green apple

1½ cups (1½ oz/45 g) spinach

Knob of ginger

8 kale leaves

4 large carrots

1 tablespoon coconut oil

Cut the apple to fit the juicer.
Place the apple, spinach, ginger,
kale, and carrots into the feeder
of a juice extractor, and run the
machine. Pour the juice into a
glass, stir in the coconut oil,
and enjoy as soon as possible.

Makes about 2 cups
(16 fl oz/500 ml)

Apple-Spinach Harmony

1 lemon

2½ green apples

1 pear

1½ cups (1½ oz/45 g) spinach

1 celery stalk

Peel the lemon and cut the lemon, apples, and pear to fit the juicer. Place the lemon, apples, pear, spinach, and celery into the feeder of a juice extractor, and run the machine. Enjoy as soon as possible.

Makes about 2 cups (16 fl oz/500 ml)

Triple Greens

½ head romaine lettuce

½ bunch kale or collard greens

1 cup (1 oz/30 g) spinach

½ bunch fresh flat-leaf parsley

2 celery stalks

1 tablespoon coconut oil

Place the romaine, kale or collards, spinach, parsley, and celery into the feeder of a juice extractor, and run the machine. Pour the juice into a glass, stir in the coconut oil, and enjoy as soon as possible.

Makes about 2 cups (16 fl oz/500 ml)

Garden Juice

1 lemon

2 apples

1 bunch kale

Knob of ginger

3 celery stalks

2 carrots

Peel the lemon. Cut the lemon and apples to fit the juicer. Place the lemon, apples, kale, ginger, celery, and carrots into the feeder of a juice extractor, and run the machine. Enjoy as soon as possible.

Makes about 2 cups (16 fl oz/500 ml)

Sweet Carrot Milk

1 cup (8 fl oz/2509 ml) hazelnut milk (page 61)

2 sweet potatoes

4 carrots

Make the hazelnut milk as directed. Cut the sweet potatoes to fit the juicer. Place the sweet potatoes and carrots into the feeder of a juice extractor, and run the machine. Pour the juice into a glass, stir in the hazelnut milk, and enjoy as soon as possible.

Makes about 2 cups (16 fl oz/500 ml)

brazil nut milk
2 mangoes
¼ pineapple

TROPICAL BOOST

Make the Brazil nut milk as
directed on page 61 to yield 1 cup
(8 fl oz/250 ml). Peel and pit the
mangoes. Peel the pineapple. Cut
the pineapple to fit the juicer.
Place the mango and pineapple into
the feeder of a juice extractor
and run the machine. Pour the
juice into a glass, mix in the
Brazil nut milk, and enjoy as soon
as possible.

❧

Makes about 2 cups
(16 fl oz/500 ml)

Sweet Beet

1 cup (8 fl oz/250 ml)
Brazil nut milk (page 61)

2 bananas

1 orange

1 golden beet

8 kale leaves

Make the brazil nut milk as directed.
Peel the bananas and orange. Cut the
orange and beet to fit the juicer.
Place the beet, kale leaves, bananas
and orange into the feeder of a juice
extractor and run the machine. Pour
the juice into a glass, mix in the nut
milk, and enjoy as soon as possible.

Makes about 2 cups (16 fl oz/500 ml)

Apple Pie

1 cup (8 fl oz/250 ml)
Brazil nut milk (page 61)

2 apples

Knob of ginger

6 carrots

Pinch of ground cinnamon

Make the Brazil nut milk as directed.
Cut the apples to fit the juicer. Place
the apples, ginger, and carrots into the
feeder of a juice extractor, and run the
machine. Pour the juice into a glass,
mix in the nut milk and cinnamon,
and enjoy as soon as possible.

Makes about 2 cups
(16 fl oz/500 ml)

Berries + Cream

1 cup (8 fl oz/250 ml)
Brazil nut milk (right)

2 bananas

2 cups (16 fl oz/500 ml)
strawberries

2 cups (16 fl oz/500 ml)
blueberries

Make the Brazil nut milk as directed. Peel the bananas. Place the strawberries, bananas, and blueberries into the feeder of a juice extractor, and run the machine. Pour the juice into a glass, stir in the Brazil nut milk, and enjoy as soon as possible.

Makes about 2 cups (16 fl oz/500 ml)

Basic Nut Milk

½ cup (2½ oz/75 g) nuts
(such as almonds, Brazil nuts,
cashews, or hazelnuts)

1 cup (8 fl oz/250 ml) filtered
water, plus more for soaking

½ tablespoon maple syrup
(optional)

Pinch of salt (optional)

Soak the nuts in a bowl of water for at least 5 hours and up to 24 hours. Drain the nuts, then place the nuts and the 1 cup (8 fl oz/250 ml) water into the feeder of a juice extractor, and run the machine. Pour the milk into a glass, stir in the maple syrup and salt, if using, and enjoy as soon as possible.

Makes about 1 cup (8 fl oz/250 ml)

Mexican Chocolate Milk

2 cups (16 fl oz/500 ml)
hazelnut milk (above right)

2 tablespoons cacao powder

Pinch of cayenne pepper

3 tablespoons raw honey

Pinch of ground cinnamon

Make the hazelnut milk as directed. Mix together the hazelnut milk, cacao powder, cayenne, honey, and cinnamon, pour into a glass, and enjoy as soon as possible.

Makes about 2 cups (16 fl oz/500 ml)

Nutty-Fruity Fueler

1 cup (8 fl oz/250 ml)
hazelnut milk (above)

1 small sweet potato

5 carrots

1 cup (4 oz/125 g) cranberries

Pinch of ground cinnamon

Make the hazelnut milk as directed. Cut the sweet potato to fit the juicer. Place the sweet potato, carrots, and cranberries into the feeder of a juice extractor, and run the machine. Pour the juice into a glass. Stir in the hazelnut milk and cinnamon, and enjoy as soon as possible.

Makes about 2 cups (16 fl oz/500 ml)

Vegetable Power Juice

½ lemon

2 apples

½ Persian cucumber

2 cups (2 oz/60 g) spinach

6 kale leaves

Knob of ginger

4 celery stalks

Peel the lemon. Cut the lemon, apples, and cucumber to fit the juicer. Place the lemon, apples, cucumber, spinach, kale, ginger, and celery into the feeder of a juice extractor, and run the machine. Enjoy as soon as possible.

Makes about 2 cups (16 fl oz/500 ml)

Deep Green Treatment

1 orange

2 beets

1 cup (2 oz/60 g) broccoli pieces

8 kale leaves

½ bunch fresh parsley

1 tablespoon coconut oil

Peel the orange and cut the orange and beets to fit the juicer. Place the broccoli, orange, kale, parsley, and beets into the feeder of a juice extractor, and run the machine. Pour the juice into a glass, stir in the coconut oil, and enjoy as soon as possible.

Makes about 2 cups (16 fl oz/500 ml)

Dark Green Infusion

1 orange

1 avocado

2 green apples

1 small sweet potato

½ Persian cucumber

2 cups (6 oz/185 g) chopped cabbage

1 small jalapeño

Peel the orange and avocado and remove the avocado pit. Cut the orange, apples, sweet potato, cucumber, and cabbage to fit the juicer. Place the apples, sweet potato, cabbage, orange, jalapeño, avocado, and cucumber into the feeder of a juice extractor, and run the machine. Enjoy as soon as possible.

Makes about 2 cups (16 fl oz/500 ml)

Super Salad

2 Persian cucumbers

1 apple

6 kale leaves

2 cups (2 oz/60 g) spinach

3 stalks celery

3 carrots

Cut the cucumbers and apple to fit the juicer. Place the kale, spinach, cucumbers, celery, carrots, and apple into the feeder of a juice extractor and run the machine. Enjoy as soon as possible.

Makes about 2 cups (16 fl oz/500 ml)

DETOX

In This Chapter

juices that DETOXIFY

Maybe you went just a little overboard, indulging in a few too many rich foods and alcoholic drinks? Consuming a bit too much happens to the best of us, especially during holidays and celebratory events. Luckily, juices can be a remedy. Detoxifying juices are designed with ingredients that boost liver and digestive functions, to help flush out toxins as well as replenish your system with Vitamin B, which is depleted while consuming alcohol or processed foods. These nutrient-dense, electrolyte-packed drinks replace toxins with an abundant variety of vitamins and minerals to keep your system strong while it cleanses. Citrus, spices, chiles, and colorful vegetables keep the combinations delicious and varied.

There are two main focuses to a detoxifying drink: to hydrate, restoring electrolytes and helping to flush out your system; and to invigorate, triggering your body's detoxification process. Adding coconut water or plain old H_2O helps dilute intense flavors in juice, restore hydration, and act as a beneficial diuretic. Fresh chiles, garlic, ginger, and warming spices are all great for kick-starting the detoxification process. Because of their heat, they awaken your digestive system, get blood flowing, and introduce a multitude of antioxidants to keep your body in tune. A hearty handful of fruits and vegetables, such as liver-detoxifying beets and antiseptic tomatoes, are added to these juices to keep things balanced and colorful.

For more on ingredients that help detoxify your system, turn to page 68.

detoxifying
INGREDIENTS

chiles

Capsaicin, the active
component that gives chiles
their fiery taste, is known
to help speed digestion,
clear upper-body congestion,
help reduce cholesterol, and
relieve head and joint aches.
Plus, it adds a nice bite
to your favorite juice.

tomatoes

Tomato juice has been known
to reduce cholesterol and
work as a natural antiseptic.
The acidity in tomatoes helps
activate the liver, which plays
a key role in detoxifying.

ginger

Ginger has been shown to relax and soothe the intestinal tract, while promoting the elimination of internal toxins.

coconut water

Like plain H_2O, coconut water works as a diuretic to help flush toxins out of the system, while also keeping the body hydrated. Non-concentrate coconut water can help with rehydration, since it's full of electrolytes. It also adds a subtle, natural sweetness to juice blends.

melons

Nearly 90 percent water, watermelons and other melons are also rich in nutrients and low in calories. Watermelons are high in vitamin C and contain the antioxidant lycopene. Cantaloupe and honeydew boast vitamins C, B and A, as well as potassium.

lemons + limes

Citrus is a great source of vitamin C, which can help to boost the immune system and provide natural energy. Both fruits add a refreshing zing to drinks. Meyer lemons are a great choice for added natural sweetness.

Sweet Escape

4 mandarin oranges

1 lime

6 guavas

1 cup (4 oz/125 g) strawberries

Peel the oranges and lime. Cut the oranges, lime, and guavas to fit the juicer. Place the oranges, lime, guavas, and strawberries into the feeder of a juice extractor, and run the machine. Enjoy as soon as possible.

Makes about 2 cups (16 fl oz/500 ml)

Lime-Coco-Melon

½ seedless watermelon, about 1 lb (500 g)

1 lime

1 teaspoon raw honey

¼ cup (2 fl oz/60 ml) coconut water

Peel the watermelon and lime and cut to fit the juicer. Place the watermelon and lime into the feeder of a juice extractor, and run the machine. Pour the juice into a glass, stir in the honey and coconut water, and enjoy as soon as possible.

Makes about 2 cups (16 fl oz/500 ml)

Red Chia Punch

2 cups (10 oz/315 g) watermelon pieces

1 lemon

2 cups (8 oz/250 g) strawberries

Knob of ginger

1 tablespoon chia seeds

Peel the watermelon and the lemon and cut to fit the juicer. Place the watermelon, strawberries, ginger, and lemon into the feeder of a juice extractor, and run the machine. Pour the juice into a glass, stir in the chia seeds, and enjoy as soon as possible.

Makes about 2 cups (16 fl oz/500 ml)

Superfood Detox

1 orange

1 cup (5 oz/155 g) watermelon pieces

1 beet

2 cups (8 oz/250 g) pomegranate seeds

1 pt (8 oz/250 g) raspberries

Peel the orange and watermelon. Cut the orange, watermelon, and beet to fit the juicer. Place the orange, watermelon, beet, pomegranate seeds, and raspberries, into the feeder of a juice extractor, and run the machine. Enjoy as soon as possible.

Makes about 2 cups (16 fl oz/500 ml)

1 lime
3 tomatoes
2 cucumbers
1 beet

DEEP RED POTION

Peel the lime. Cut the lime,
tomatoes, cucumbers, and
beet to fit the juicer.
Place the lime, tomatoes,
cucumbers, and beet into the
feeder of a juice extractor,
and run the machine. Enjoy
as soon as possible.

Makes about 2 cups
(16 fl oz/500 ml)

Tropical Virgin Mary

- ¼ pineapple
- 2 tomatoes
- 1 small piece fresh horseradish, or 1 tablespoon prepared horseradish
- 2 celery stalks
- ¼ bunch fresh parsley
- ½ head red leaf lettuce

Peel the pineapple and cut the pineapple and tomatoes to fit the juicer. Place the pineapple, horseradish, celery, parsley, lettuce, and tomatoes into the feeder of a juice extractor, and run the machine. Enjoy as soon as possible.

Makes about 2 cups (16 fl oz/500 ml)

Tomato Salad-in-a-Glass

- 1 lime
- 3 tomatoes
- 2 cucumbers
- 8 kale leaves
- 3 stalks celery

Peel the lime. Cut the lime, tomatoes, and cucumbers to fit the juicer. Place the lime, tomatoes, cucumbers, kale, and celery into the feeder of a juice extractor, and run the machine. Enjoy as soon as possible.

Makes about 2 cups (16 fl oz/500 ml)

Super Detox Elixir

1 lemon

2 green apples

1 cucumber

1 beet

Knob of ginger

3 stalks celery

Peel the lemon. Cut the lemon, apples, cucumber, and beet to fit the juicer. Place the lemon, apples, cucumber, beet, ginger, and celery into the feeder of a juice extractor, and run the machine. Enjoy as soon as possible.

Makes about 2 cups (16 fl oz/500 ml)

Carrot Booster

1 clove garlic

Knob of ginger

1 head red leaf lettuce

8 carrots

Peel the garlic. Place the garlic, ginger, lettuce, and carrots into the feeder of a juice extractor, and run the machine. Enjoy as soon as possible.

Makes about 2 cups (16 fl oz/500 ml)

Electrolyte Balancer

1 lime

2 apples

1 cucumber

½ bulb fennel

8 kale leaves

1 cup (8 fl oz/250 ml) coconut water

Peel the lime and cut the lime, apples, cucumber, and fennel to fit the juicer. Place the lime, apples, fennel, kale, and cucumber into the feeder of a juice extractor, and run the machine. Pour the juice into a glass, stir in the coconut water, and enjoy as soon as possible.

Makes about 2 cups (16 fl oz/500 ml)

Anti-inflammatory Tonic

1 cantaloupe

1 lime

1 small fresh turmeric

½ jalapeño

8 basil leaves

1 cup (8 fl oz/250 ml) coconut water

Peel and seed the cantaloupe. Peel the lime. Cut the cantaloupe and lime to fit the juicer. Place the cantaloupe, turmeric, jalapeño, basil, and lime into the feeder of a juice extractor, and run the machine. Pour the juice into a glass, stir in the coconut water, and enjoy as soon as possible.

Makes about 2 cups (16 fl oz/500 ml)

2 meyer lemons
6 asian pears
knob of ginger

GINGER-ASIAN PEAR

Makes
about 2 cups
(16 fl oz/
500 ml)

Peel the lemons and cut
the lemons and pears to
fit the juicer. Place
the pears, ginger, and
lemons into the feeder of
a juice extractor, and
run the machine. Enjoy
as soon as possible.

Spicy Apple-Cucumber

- 1 lemon
- 4 green apples
- 1 Persian cucumber
- 1 small hot red chile
- Knob of ginger

Peel the lemon and cut the lemon, apples, and cucumber to fit the juicer. Place the lemon, apples, chile, ginger, and cucumber into the feeder of a juice extractor, and run the machine. Enjoy as soon as possible.

Makes about 2 cups (16 fl oz/500 ml)

Gingery Roots + Apple

- 3 beets
- 1 apple
- 3 large carrots
- Knob of ginger
- ½ cup (½ oz/15 g) spinach or kale

Cut the beets and apple to fit the juicer. Place the beets, carrots, ginger, spinach, and apple into the feeder of a juice extractor, and run the machine. Enjoy as soon as possible.

Makes about 2 cups (16 fl oz/500 ml)

Mango-Coconut Agua Fresca

4 mangoes

1 lime

1 cup (8 fl oz/250 ml)
coconut water

Peel the mangoes and remove the pits.
Peel the lime and cut it to fit the
juicer. Place the mangoes and lime into
the feeder of a juice extractor, and
run the machine. Pour the juice into
a glass, stir in the coconut water,
and enjoy as soon as possible.

Makes about 2 cups (16 fl oz/500 ml)

Spiced Orange-Beet

2 oranges

2 red beets

Knob of ginger

3 carrots

Pinch of cayenne

Peel the oranges and cut the oranges
and beets to fit the juicer. Place the
oranges, beets, ginger, and carrots
into the feeder of a juice extractor,
and run the machine. Pour the juice
into a glass, stir in the cayenne,
and enjoy as soon as possible.

Makes about 2 cups (16 fl oz/500 ml)

Beet-Apple-Coconut

4 red apples

3 red beets

1 cup (8 fl oz/250 ml)
coconut water

Cut the apples and beets to fit the
juicer. Place the apples and beets
into the feeder of a juice extractor,
and run the machine. Pour the juice
into a glass, stir in the coconut
water, and enjoy as soon as possible.

Makes about 2 cups (16 fl oz/500 ml)

Spinach-Parsley Purifier

1 lemon

3 green apples

4 cups (4 oz/120 g) spinach

1 bunch fresh parsley

½ jalapeño

Peel the lemon and cut the lemon and
apples to fit the juicer. Place the
apples, spinach, parsley, jalapeño,
and lemon into the feeder of a juice
extractor, and run the machine.
Enjoy as soon as possible.

Makes about 2 cups (16 fl oz/500 ml)

1 papaya
¼ pineapple
1 jalapeño
1 pear

TROPICAL SPICE

Peel the papaya and
pineapple. Cut the
papaya, pineapple, and
pear to fit the juicer.
Place the papaya,
pineapple, jalapeño, and
pear into the feeder
of a juice extractor, and
run the machine. Enjoy
as soon as possible.

Makes about 2 cups
(16 fl oz/500 ml)

Spicy Melon Elixir

½ watermelon

1 serrano chile

8 fresh basil leaves

½ cup (4 fl oz/125 g)
coconut water

Peel the watermelon and cut to fit the
juicer. Place the watermelon, chile,
and basil into the feeder of a juice
extractor, and run the machine. Pour the
juice into a glass, mix in the coconut
water, and enjoy as soon as possible.

Makes about 2 cups (16 fl oz/500 ml)

Citrus Detoxifier

2 grapefruits

2 oranges

1 large piece of aloe plant

1 jalapeño

Peel the grapefruits and oranges and cut
to fit in the juicer. Place the grapefruits,
aloe, jalapeño, and oranges into the
feeder of a juice extractor, and run the
machine. Enjoy as soon as possible.

Makes about 2 cups (16 fl oz/500 ml)

Hangover Cure

1 medium watermelon

1 lime

1 cucumber

Knob of ginger

Peel the watermelon and lime and cut the watermelon, lime, and cucumber to fit the juicer. Place the watermelon, lime, ginger, and cucumber into the feeder of a juice extractor, and run the machine. Enjoy as soon as possible.

Makes about 2 cups (16 fl oz/500 ml)

Orange Zinger

2 ripe fuyu persimmons

Knob of ginger

1 small fresh turmeric

1 cup (4 oz/125 g) pomegranate seeds

4 carrots

Remove the stems from the persimmons and cut to fit the juicer. Place the persimmons, ginger, turmeric, pomegranate seeds, and carrots into the feeder of a juice extractor, and run the machine. Enjoy as soon as possible.

Makes about 2 cups (16 fl oz/500 ml)

Light + Bright

1 small honeydew melon

1 lime

1 orange

1 Persian cucumber

1 large piece aloe plant

Peel and seed the melon. Peel the lime and orange. Cut the melon, lime, orange, and cucumber to fit the juicer. Place the melon, lime, orange, aloe, and cucumber into the feeder of a juice extractor, and run the machine. Enjoy as soon as possible.

Makes about 2 cups (16 fl oz/500 ml)

Carrot-Apple-Ginger

1 lemon

3 green apples

Knob of ginger

5 carrots

Peel the lemon and cut the lemon and apples to fit the juicer. Place the lemon, apples, ginger, and carrots into the feeder of a juice extractor, and run the machine. Enjoy as soon as possible.

Makes about 2 cups (16 fl oz/500 ml)

PROTECT

In This Chapter

juices that PROTECT

These immunity-boosting elixirs are perhaps the most vital type of juice to incorporate into a diet. Protecting our bodies means making them strong enough to fight against germs, destructive bone, organ, and blood diseases, and the wear-and-tear of stress and missed sleep. These drinks make excellent daily supplements to keep your immune system strong, but are also great to drink before and after physically demanding events. Juices with immune-boosting qualities can help safeguard you through cold and flu season, keep your body balanced through intense travel or emotionally taxing times, and protect your organs and bones from natural, or exercise-induced deterioration.

When you're deciding what to put in a protective juice, think of produce that holds certain associations. For example, carrots are associated with good eyesight and citrus with high levels of vitamin C. Toss those in there! Pair them with disease-fighting, antioxidant-rich berries, like pomegranates and blueberries, along with generous amounts of immune system-boosters, like fresh ginger and chiles, which fight infection. Don't limit these drinks for just the bad times—keep them in your daily routine to aid your health all year long. Instead of waiting until you feel stressed or are getting sick, make juicing a lifestyle to help you feel strong and healthy anytime!

For more on ingredients that protect the immune system, turn to page 90.

protecting
INGREDIENTS

pomegranates

The juice of these tree fruits contains powerful antioxidant substances that protect cells from oxidation. They are also a good source of vitamin C, which is known to support the immune system.

oranges

Citrus fruits are rich in vitamin C and potassium, both of which have been shown to boost the immune system and help ward off illness.

blueberries

These dark colored fruits are a powerful source of antioxidants that have been linked to improved memory. They are also rich in flavonoids, which help protect against cancer and contribute to heart health.

chiles

Hot chiles, such as jalapeños, serranos, and Thai chiles, are high in vitamins A and C, which have been known to prevent infections and boost the immune system.

carrots

Carrots are not just good for your eyes, they've also been known to lower risks of cancer and arthritis. Carrots are high in vitamin A, beta carotene, and good-for-you carotenoids.

Blueberry Blast

- 1 grapefruit
- 1 lime
- 2 apples
- 2 cups (8 oz/250 g) blueberries
- 2 carrots

Peel the grapefruit and lime and cut the grapefruit, lime, and apples to fit the juicer. Place the grapefruit, lime, apples, blueberries, and carrots into the feeder of a juice extractor, and run the machine. Enjoy as soon as possible.

Makes about 2 cups (16 fl oz/500 ml)

Antioxidant Potion

- ½ lemon
- 5 tomatoes
- 1 Persian cucumber
- 1 celery stalk
- 1 carrots

Peel the lemon. Cut the tomatoes and cucumber to fit the juicer. Place the lemon, tomatoes, cucumber, celery, and carrots into the feeder of a juice extractor, and run the machine. Enjoy as soon as possible.

Makes about 2 cups (16 fl oz/500 ml)

Rabbit Fuel

- 2 oranges
- 4 celery stalks
- 4 carrots

Peel the oranges and cut to fit the juicer. Place the oranges, celery, and carrots into the feeder of a juice extractor and run the machine. Enjoy as soon as possible.

Makes about 2 cups (16 fl oz/500 ml)

Heart Helper

- ½ lime
- 2 red bell peppers
- 1 tomato
- 1 Persian cucumber
- 1 jalapeño

Peel the lime. Cut the peppers, tomato, and cucumber to fit the juicer. Place the lime, peppers, tomato, jalapeño, and cucumber into the feeder of a juice extractor, and run the machine. Enjoy as soon as possible.

Makes about 2 cups (16 fl oz/500 ml)

2 pomegranates
1 grapefruit
knob of ginger
4 carrots

POTENT PROTECTOR

Cold Thwarter

- 2 oranges
- 1 lime
- 1 mango
- 2 cups (8 oz/250 g) pomegranate seeds
- ½ jalapeño

Peel the citrus and cut to fit the juicer. Peel and pit the mango. Place the oranges, lime, seeds, jalapeño, and mango into the feeder of a juice extractor, and run the machine. Enjoy as soon as possible.

Makes about 2 cups (16 fl oz/500 ml)

Ginger-Berry-Pom

- 2 tangerines
- 2 red apples
- 2 cups (8 oz/250 g) pomegranate seeds
- 2 cups (8 oz/250 g) raspberries
- Knob of ginger

Peel the tangerines. Cut the apples to fit the juicer. Place the apples, pomegranate seeds, raspberries, ginger, and tangerines into the feeder of a juice extractor, and run the machine. Enjoy as soon as possible.

Makes about 2 cups (16 fl oz/500 ml)

Remove the seeds from the pomegranates. Peel the grapefruit and cut to fit the juicer. Place the pomegranate seeds, grapefruit, ginger, and carrots into the feeder of a juice extractor, and run the machine. Enjoy as soon as possible.

Makes about 2 cups (16 fl oz/500 ml)

5-ingredient Fighter

- 1 mango
- 1 lime
- 1 orange
- ¼ pineapple
- 10 fresh mint leaves

Peel the mango and remove the pit. Peel the lime, orange, and pineapple and cut to fit the juicer. Place the mango, lime, orange, mint, and pineapple into the feeder of a juice extractor, and run the machine. Enjoy as soon as possible.

Makes about 2 cups (16 fl oz/500 ml)

Simple Citrus-Beet

- 4 oranges
- 3 red beets

Peel the oranges and cut the oranges and beets to fit the juicer. Place the oranges and beets into the feeder of a juice extractor, and run the machine. Enjoy as soon as possible.

Makes about 2 cups (16 fl oz/500 ml)

Tropical Tonic

- 3 papayas
- 1 lime
- 1 mango

Peel the papayas and lime and cut to fit the juicer. Peel the mango and remove the pit. Place the papaya, lime, and mango into the feeder of a juice extractor, and run the machine. Enjoy as soon as possible.

Makes about 2 cups (16 fl oz/500 ml)

Honeydew-Kiwi Cooler

- ½ honeydew melon
- 4 kiwis
- 1 lime

Peel the melon, kiwis, and lime and cut to fit the juicer. Place the melon, kiwi, and lime into the feeder of a juice extractor, and run the machine. Enjoy as soon as possible.

Makes about 2 cups (16 fl oz/500 ml)

BERRY-POM

3 pomegranates
2 pt blackberries
2 pt blueberries

Seed the pomegranates. Place
the pomegranate seeds,
blackberries, and blueberries
(or 2 pt/16 oz/500 g total
mixed berries) into the
feeder of a juice extractor,
and run the machine. Enjoy
as soon as possible.

Makes about 2 cups
(16 fl oz/500 ml)

Berry Supreme

- 1 cup (4 oz/125 g) raspberries
- 1 cup (4 oz/125 g) blueberries
- 1 cup (4 oz/125 g) fresh or thawed, frozen cranberries
- 1 cup (8 fl oz/250 ml) coconut water
- 2 tablespoons raw honey

Place raspberries, blueberries, and cranberries into the feeder of a juice extractor, and run the machine. Pour the juice into a glass, stir in the coconut water and honey, and enjoy as soon as possible.

Makes about 2 cups (16 fl oz/500 ml)

Recharger

- 2 oranges
- 2 tangerines
- 2 cups (8 oz/250 g) blueberries
- 2 tablespoons chia seeds

Peel the oranges and tangerines and cut to fit the juicer. Place the blueberries, oranges, and tangerines into the feeder of a juice extractor, and run the machine. Pour the juice into a glass, stir in the chia seeds, and enjoy as soon as possible.

Makes about 2 cups (16 fl oz/500 ml)

1 orange
½ lemon
¼ pineapple
2 carrots

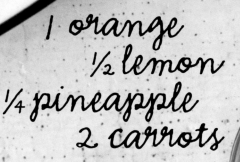

CARROT SUNRISE

Peel the orange, lemon, and pineapple
and cut to fit the juicer.
Place the orange, lemon, pineapple,
and carrots into the feeder of a
juice extractor, and run the machine.
Enjoy as soon as possible.

Makes about 2 cups
(16 fl oz/500 ml)

Carrot-Wheatgrass

2 containers wheatgrass
(about 2 cups/2 oz/60 g)
when trimmed

8 carrots

Place the wheatgrass and carrots
into the feeder of a juice
extractor, and run the machine.
Enjoy as soon as possible.

Makes about 2 cups
(16 fl oz/500 ml)

Orange Boost

1 lemon

1 orange

1 papaya

1 small fresh turmeric

Knob of ginger

8 carrots

Peel the lemon, orange, and papaya
and cut to fit the juicer. Place the
lemon, orange, papaya, turmeric,
ginger, and carrots into the feeder
of a juice extractor, and run the
machine. Enjoy as soon as possible.

Makes about 2 cups
(16 fl oz/500 ml)

Brassica Bomb

1 lemon

2 pears

2 apples

2 cups (6 oz/185 g) chopped cabbage

8 kale leaves

Peel the lemon and cut the lemon, pears, and apples to fit the juicer. Place the lemon, pears, cabbage, kale and apples into the feeder of a juice extractor, and run the machine. Enjoy as soon as possible.

Makes about 2 cups (16 fl oz/500 ml)

Cherry Zinger

2 tangerines

1 lemon

2 apples

1 cup (6 oz/185 g) pitted fresh or thawed, frozen sweet cherries

5 carrots

Peel the tangerines and lemon. Cut the tangerines, lemon, and apples to fit the juicer. Place the tangerines, apples, cherries, carrots, and lemon into the feeder of a juice extractor, and run the machine. Enjoy as soon as possible.

Makes about 2 cups (16 fl oz/500 ml)

Spicy Ps

1 papaya

¼ pineapple

1 pear

1 jalapeño

Peel the papaya and pineapple. Cut the papaya, pineapple, and pear to fit the juicer. Place the papaya, pineapple, jalapeño, and pear into the feeder of a juice extractor, and run the machine. Enjoy as soon as possible.

Makes about 2 cups (16 fl oz/500 ml)

Cranberry-Pear Tonic

3 pears

2½ cups (10 oz/315 g) fresh or thawed, frozen cranberries

Cut the pears to fit the juicer. Place the pears and cranberries into the feeder of a juice extractor, and run the machine. Enjoy as soon as possible.

Makes about 2 cups (16 fl oz/ 500 ml)

INDEX

weldonowen

1045 Sansome Street, Suite 100, San Francisco, CA 94111
Telephone: 415 291 0100 Fax: 415 291 8841
www.weldonowen.com

Weldon Owen is a division of

BONNIER

WELDON OWEN, INC.
CEO and President Terry Newell
VP, Sales and Marketing Amy Kaneko
VP, Publisher Roger Shaw
Director of Finance Philip Paulick

Associate Publisher Jennifer Newens
Assistant Editor Emma Rudolph

Creative Director Kelly Booth
Art Director Alisha Petro
Designer Rachel Lopez Metzger

Production Director Chris Hemesath
Associate Production Director Michelle Duggan

Photographer Sara Remington
Food Stylist Erin Quon
Prop Stylist Christine Wolheim

Location Oak Hill Farm of Sonoma
Models Jessica Kane, Leonard Mueller,
Hilary Seeley

Printed and bound by 1010 Printing, Ltd. in China

First printed in 2014
10 9 8 7 6 5

Library of Congress Control Number: 2014930805
ISBN-13: 978-1-61628-683-5
ISBN-10: 1-61628-683-0

ACKNOWLEDGMENTS
Weldon Owen wishes to thank Debbie Berne, Malinda DeRouen Mueller,
Doug Mueller, Lori Nunokawa, Nicole Rejwan, and Krysia Zaroda
for their generous support in producing this book.